The PHANTOM in Management

by

MARJORIE L. ELLIS

authorHOUSE

1663 LIBERTY DRIVE, SUITE 200
BLOOMINGTON, INDIANA 47403
(800) 839-8640
www.authorhouse.com

First published by AuthorHouse 04/09/05

ISBN: 1-4184-3901-0 (e)
ISBN: 1-4184-3900-2 (sc)

Printed in the United States of America
Bloomington, Indiana

This book is printed on acid-free paper.

DEDICATION

This manual could only be dedicated to my husband and best friend, William H. Ellis (Bill). Bill's encouragement and belief in this concept was my greatest motivation for completing this project.

Marjorie L. Ellis

MEMO

To: The Reader

From: The Author

Your selection of this manual will challenge your present understanding of full-cycle management. This is the result of more than two decades of management training in private business, research, and government administration by awesome administrative professionals. As you can imagine, there are many entertaining stories and insights that would be great fun to share with you (and very tempting to tell). However, since my objective is to get you straight to the point, I have condensed the manual as though I had completed the SPEED READING for you. You will find that only the explanations of my trial and error work progression is used to bring about your understanding quickly of the MISSING LINK IN MANAGEMENT.

If all who read this manual will adjust their management style to include this missing link in management, there would be an instantaneous surge of communications and a definite inability for fraud in most areas of business. Also, productivity and quality control would be the by-product of this adjustment.

As you might surmise, I have great enthusiasm for this manual and believe that its concept should be incorporated into every office training program.

TABLE OF CONTENTS

Section 1.

INTRODUCTION...

Notes:

INTRODUCTION

This manual could easily be placed under the 'MYSTERY' section within Book Stores and Libraries except for the fact that it is not fiction. The title does, however, suggest the mystery of the subject. Hopefully, your inquiring mind and sense of adventure will be all that is necessary to get you and other managers curious enough to take an hour break and discover the mystery and how it will impact your careers and life as you incorporate this missing link in management.

It was very obvious throughout my career that most people (even most managers) do not see the 'whole picture' in the delicate area of management. Only after retirement did I actually begin to understand what was missing in management. The progression of my education in this phenomenon is in essence the style in which "The Phantom in Management" was written.

The name "The Phantom in Management" was chosen because the missing link in management eluded me for over twenty years. In retrospect, I actually performed a twenty-year pilot program in the study of MANAGEMENT. A bibliography mode of presentation shows not only the mystery of the missing link in management, but also will train the READER while following my progression. The reader will be able to apply this knowledge to his specific needs.

You have been trained by many excellent professors or on-the-job training programs to become successful managers. What they did not understand is what you have missed. The answer lies very close to the surface, yet has for the most part remained hidden for nearly fifty years.

The irony connected to all organized management today has been their efforts to control by layers of administrative professionals. Their concept seems to be that more is better. You will find this scenario present in Local, State and Federal Governments, Industries, and surprisingly, also in the private sector. No doubt, you have heard on the news that private businesses seem to have less managerial problems than their corporate counterparts. There is a logical explanation for this truth. Although, we hear these types of statements on television daily, most of us will not investigate the source or question the truth of them.

When you are meeting with top executives or administrators, a similar conversation will emerge, "After all the budgeting, planning, and man hours have been completed, some facet of the original plan . . . went astray. We are convinced that the original plan was correct, but John Doe let the ball drop which altered the plan causing our problem in quality control and many of our production overruns." As an objective bystander, you would have probably wondered why someone did not see John Doe drop the ball. Obviously, the answer to your question would be that NO ONE WAS WATCHING.

Having stated the obvious, NO ONE WAS WATCHING, what was your immediate reaction? Maybe . . . who was delegated to monitor the progress of the program or project? Over the years, I have found that most management personnel could immediately place the ultimate blame on a particular person or department. This is understandable, because most of the time (after-the-fact) the problem can be traced to a point of origin.

It seems that it has become professionally correct to establish goals, set schedules to a point of conclusion, then continue with our daily duties until 'out-of-the-blue' someone stumbles over the fact that things have gone astray. Even though the professional is paid to get the job done, most of the time the professional is ONLY watching his area of expertise. The reason we fail to catch the problems as they occur, is because we do not have a completely different area or person figured into the equation. To complete full-cycle management, there must always be a connecting mechanism or PERSON in charge of continuity.

Numerous books have been published and seminars presented to guide Executives and Administrators through TOTAL QUALITY MANAGEMENT and QUALITY CONTROL. These have been at great expense. As great as these concepts have proven to be, you will still hear at some time during a conference or over a business luncheon . . . "The budget monies where approved, the most qualified and best trained professionals in place, the planning unique, but John Doe dropped the ball. By the time the problems surfaced, we came up short of the original desired results or product." These conversations usually take on a climate of 'fault finding' and most of the time upper management has someone or a department in which to place the responsibility for this problem. Having made this statement, I would like to defend upper management because they are just doing their job as it was done before them. Frankly, only after I reached my understanding of what is really the missing link in management could I have so generously defended their actions.

As you already have experienced, when these errors or disastrous problems surface, the scramble to modify in mid-stream is the normal procedure to salvage the product or project. The 'normal' procedure has been detrimental to Governmental Agencies, Corporations, and Businesses. Billions of misspent dollars are wasted each year to correct this 'normal' procedure and almost always produces an inferior result.

We do not usually connect our private lives in the same category as business. However, this phenomenon has also affected our churches, homes, and schools. While pondering over the impact of the missing link in management, I realized that the same communication problems exist throughout all areas of our lives.

In our churches, we witness a lack of communication that causes misunderstandings and discouragement. One committee does not understand the need for the other committees to be aware of their actions or many times the same information or programs are duplicated because of this disregard of communications. Only after the errors are found or misunderstandings have festered is there an awareness of a problem. This can cause members and Pastors to leave. Many churches have split because of the heighten pitch of these misunderstandings which in most cases have been brought about because of communication problems. Therefore, the church became disconnected.

In our homes, we are witnessing the cruel effects of not being connected to each other. Someone has to be in charge of the schedules of our children, their appointments and activities. Many problems arise from a lack of communications, and it is especially crucial to be aware of CHANGES in schedules for their welfare, stability, and safety. Parents are struggling with the disastrous results of not being connected to their children in many areas of their lives. This problem surfaced when our society became a two-paycheck household. That left most families without that one PERSON who was available to keep the lines of communications open.

In our schools, problems have escalated and seem in some areas of the country to be out of control. However, if we could look past the individual problems and focus on the root cause, most of the time it is a breakdown of communications in one or more areas of the student's life. What we don't know about, becomes impossible to change, fix, or address. It is difficult for parents to be connected to the teachers and school administrators. It is equally difficult for teacher and school administrators to be connected with the students family. Add to this equation . . . the proper communications connecting curriculum changes, funding, adequate personnel and you have a recipe for an overwhelming task of raising and educating the masses. This lack of effective communications has already produced lower scores as well as a climate of unrest and crime on school property.

As I proceed to unravel this mystery, I believe you will also realize the connection to all the different facets as a lack of full-cycle management. It is my intent to reveal the MISSING LINK IN MANAGEMENT by mirroring my progression. Thus, simultaneously train you in a specific mind set. The information you will need to incorporate this new concept into your management style should have taken shape in your mind as you read and understand what the missing link in management encompasses. As you read, your understanding should progress as follows:

1. You will understand the simplicity of the missing link.
2. You will recognize your management area that is missing this facet.
3. You will formulate a plan to incorporate this link as soon as possible.
4. You will need to make the determination if you have a person on board or if you will need to hire.

It is difficult at this moment to visualize or accept the statements above and you are probably thinking that this seems like an over simplification. However, once you have completed this manual, you will have already formulated in your mind how to use the 1, 2, 3, and 4-step method to alter your present management style and achieve a complete TOTAL MANAGEMENT concept.

Once this concept is understood and incorporated into the full-cycle management equation, surely the next step would be for all teaching/training programs to include this concept, both business and throughout the academic sector.

I feel certain that you will find this adventure as profitable for you as it has proven to be for me!

Section 2.

IN SEARCH OF THE PHANTOM.............................

Notes:

IN SEARCH OF THE PHANTOM

The inspiration for this revelation regarding most management styles came with more astonishment to me than it probably will to you. As I attempt to outline my progression into what should have been the obvious, I am convinced that you will grasp the concept immediately. While on this journey into the simplicity of management, you will witness the arena of complexity which a growing nation and world pitched their management style in an effort to bring about TOTAL MANAGEMENT.

During the first five years of my career, I had the good fortune to work for great managers. My definition of great managers during those early years of office experience only meant that they didn't yell at me when I made those first-time mistakes that are inevitable with inexperienced employees. Nevertheless, I gained great insight into the working world at a very young age and began my growth in analytical management. Literally, I began to have a sense of office routine – what worked and what didn't. Now, you know what they say, 'a little knowledge is or can be a dangerous thing.' Well, guess what, I fell into that trap. By the time I came out of the workforce to raise a family, I honestly thought I had mastered the art of management. (Actually, this was due to the fact that I was trusted employee and my supervisors and manager allowed me to fill in for them in some instances and complete work I knew only they usually handled. I think you might call this a false sense of authority.)

DEVELOPMENT OF THE FOLLOW-UP SYSTEM

I had both of my children in school by 1969 and decided that now was the time to resume my career. At my first interview, I was offered the position of secretary to the Manager of Research and Development in a well-known tire manufacturing company. The first six months, I was totally over my head in the complexity of organizing a plan to follow all aspects of this very busy research facility. The struggle to keep up with the four project managers for the manager and the progress of all the projects for which each was responsible was the reason for the development of an adequate follow-up system.

In order to project the timely coordination of each department and project, it was necessary for me to meet with the Research Manager and Project Managers while they developed their goals and expectations into a yearly plan. It was my responsibility to present a schedule or system to keep track of each manager and project. This schedule or system would document the dates to begin the process and subsequent dates for each transaction from the laboratory, to the pilot plant, to completion and include the projected date to go into production.

A copy of the follow-up system was approved by management and then given to the project managers. The project managers were responsible for meeting all deadlines. It was my responsibility to track each project and document their dates of completion and notify ALL when these dates were not met. They would give their explanations to the Manager and new dates would be established and the schedule updated and the process would resume. Each staff member was given an updated schedule and they could adequately follow the progress of the other departments. This was important because their projects depended upon the timely completion of the other departments.

The follow-up system that I had developed gained me a raise and a sense of accomplishment that I had never experienced before. To be so completely trusted by these – in my opinion – intellectual giants was quite a boost to my ego. Now, with this inflated ego, I really thought I had 'made it.' The next four years were a continuation of this success. It was my good fortune to work in the production area of this facility for a time. I developed a similar follow-up system in the production department that also proved successful. In my reasoning, I deducted that this was confirmation that my 'famous follow-up system' would be successful in most areas of business.

It is important to understand that the follow-up system is the INSTRUMENT used to monitor the progress from the beginning to the end of a project in a methodological manner, but it is crucial that the manager understands that the system DOES NOT stand alone. SOMEONE must control or monitor the system to ensure that all areas are adequately completed or that delays (or changes) are documented and reported to ALL involved.

At the end of 1973, I realized with great concern that my family had not adjusted to my career and many noticeable changes had occurred in my children. After much deliberation, I made the decision to once again put my career on hold.

MARJORIE L. ELLIS

EXPANDING SKILLS IN ANALYTICAL MANAGEMENT

Nearly four years later, I updated my resume' and decided to look outside of industry for a different type of position. Coincidentally, a new City Manager had just been hired that week and was looking for a Secretary. He seemed very interested in my resume' and called for an interview. I was required to pass a shorthand test as part of the requirements for the position. Well, shorthand never was one of my strong points – I took the transcribed letter out of the typewriter and gave my apologies to the Secretary and left. Humiliated, I just went home. To my complete surprise, the Secretary from the City Manager's office called the next day and set up an appointment again for me to be interviewed. The Manager explained that he needed assistance from an experienced secretary with the ability to work with all departments of the City. Also, he was impressed with my scheduling experience. It was his custom in the past to use a Dictaphone and my shortcomings in dictation was not an issue.

I didn't realize at the time what a great opportunity this position was going to hold for me. Later, the Manager expanded my duties to include following up on specific projects or completion dates in many areas of the ongoing management of the City. I then began developing – once again – my style of following up that was very quickly accepted and respected by the Manager and his department managers. Expanding into budget compilation with the Manager and his departments enabled me to develop the follow-up system to a new level – different, but essentially the same process. The City Manager and Department Managers make specific goals and put dates for completion in motion. There needed to be different levels of the follow-up system, but even though there were more steps to the process, the follow-up system still worked exactly the same. The important factor about a well implemented and effective follow-up system is ALL facts or dates are monitored by the PERSON given the responsibility to follow them to the completion of the project or until the goal has been accomplished.

As I continued with what had become a well-established follow-up system, I also began compiling information in other areas and expanded my involvement within the City. This necessitated contacting agencies outside of the City. This seemed very ordinary at the time, but I later realized the significance of the confidence each agency had shown. (When you serve 'your' agenda while serving the agenda of other departments and/or agencies, a bond like no other management tool is inevitable.) There were times when I felt more like an 'information machine' than a secretary. At this point, I didn't have a clue to the actual reason for my apparent success.

While riding this stallion of cooperation, I subconsciously began perfecting the follow-up system to an art. If a project or budget schedule in the follow-up system needed ANYTHING – such as reminders, extensions, changes, revisions of any type, I was totally involved with each transaction until it was completed. This included notification of each person or department involved of 'all' transactions and updates.

Instead of covering just four departments as I did in Research and Development, the follow-up system for the City was broken into more departments, but since the City Manager allowed me to be present at many of their staff meetings, I quickly learned to segregate each department. I then organized the different projects under each department similar to the follow-up system used while in Research. There were more categories, but the system was essentially the same. (There are goals or duties and all have a schedule for completion. The follow-up system must be designed to record these goals or duties, showing their timing expectations, and MUST be documented adequately on all transactions . . . such as reminders, delays, changes, and completion dates. Notification is as important to all involved as the schedule itself.) Actually, extensive training in the Research Department gave me the foundation to adequately prepare the follow-up system for the City. It was an expansion from a four-department follow-up system to a seventeen-department follow-up system. I also found it necessary to use two categories (PLANNING and BUDGETING).

The City is multi-faceted and complex. It is necessary to follow full-cycle management in many areas. The City Manager and the City's Departments also had follow up demands with agencies outside of the City (State, Federal, and Local). The follow-up system used in these categories was formulated as the needs occurred. Even though there were multi-layers, once the system had been formulated, the success then depended upon the PERSON responsible for monitoring the system.

Within a year, the office seemed to run well even in my absence. The position seemed to have become too complacent and I began expanding into writing Policy and Procedures, developing the City's Policy and Procedure Manual, and began researching troubled areas as assigned by the City Manager. Still, I felt the position had become uneventful and stagnate.

The Manager of my former position in Research contacted me and offered to substantially increase my salary if I would return. After many agonizing days, and many conversations with my colleagues at the City and my family, I decided to take the offer. I now believe that the choice was a good one, but at the time it seemed very risky. The actual transferring of roles came very easily because of my research experience.

DEVELOPMENT OF ONE-YEAR AND FIVE-YEAR PLANS IN RESEARCH

Once the Research Manager revealed his plans to develop a one-year and a five-year plan to the Project Managers, it was up to me to get the follow-up system on line. Since I was very familiar with the department managers and many of their projects, the follow-up system seemed to be very automatic to formulate. Once the goals and timing had been established by each project manager, the progression from department to department was documented and the follow-up system was up and running. There were problems and delays, but all were properly documented and each manager involved was notified which allowed each to be addressed and adequately rectified until the Research Department had a yearly and five-year plan completed.

The next year proved to be very productive and during this period, I had been approached by the City's Finance Director to write manuals for his department. The idea of beginning in business as a Consultant and writing manuals was very intriguing.

CONSULTANT

The Director of Finance for the City was very prompt in offering me a contract to write policy and procedural manuals for the City's Accounts Payable, Accounts Receivable, and Refuse Departments.

The most rewarding aspect of this new position was the challenge of interviewing for each segment of the manuals. Interviewing is, in my opinion, like a game. There are certain facts you must have to complete the thought pattern of any position and the challenge is getting the person you are interviewing to follow each step to its conclusion. Most people are not trainers by experience and certainly not by nature. I had to take the role of training myself and if the explanation did not get me from Step A to Step B, then I had to ask the specific questions necessary to extract this information from the person I was interviewing. I can honestly say that it was one of the most challenging times of my working career.

I now understand why writing manuals usually come with such a high price tag. The work is tedious and most writers aren't going to work that hard for any length of time. The Director seemed very pleased with the manuals and accepted them on the first draft.

After I completed the manuals for the City, I took a temporary position in the Department of Social Services. This position allowed me insight into another tremendously overworked department. Since it is my nature to "fix" everything or at least to try, I began searching for a solution to their dilemma. Office revamping was obviously needed. It was evident that the need was great for a follow-up system to shorten their workload and to accomplish departmental control. After discussing my analogy with the supervisor and the staff, they unanimously agreed. The Supervisor assigned two employees to assist in the revamping of the department and complete a follow-up system. Also, updated computer printouts to include every client. The clients would be separated into either closed or open files from that point on. The supervisors and their staff totally supported our efforts and by the time I left the Agency, we were all pleased at the results.

ANALYTICAL DISCOVERY

I worked sporadically for several years until my husband retired and we began traveling. We returned home from a trip to find a message from a colleague at the Department of Social Services. I was very excited to hear from her and immediately returned her call to set a time for lunch.

Excited as I was to meet with her for lunch, I was totally shocked to hear her comments on the progress of the Agency. Only a few months after I left, the 'system' had broken down. They had to rework the staff and paperwork in order to bring about departmental control of the workload and performance standards.

In discussing this revelation with my husband . . . he remarked, "as long as you were present the follow-up system worked." Immediately, I ascertained that it wasn't the follow-up system, but the OPERATOR of the system that was the MISSING LINK IN MANAGEMENT. Thus, the concept of 'THE PHANTOM IN MANAGEMENT' was born.

Section 3.

HINDSIGHT INTO THIS PHENOMENON..................

Notes:

HINDSIGHT INTO THIS PHENOMENON

I discussed this amazing phenomenon with anyone who would listen. The broader scope of how and why we evolved into disconnected businesses had become apparent. Not only could this be found nationally, but internationally as well.

Let us use for an example the United States. When we evolved into the industrial age and began booming in all areas of business, the one common thread prevalent in all business was that each BEGAN . . . that is, they started out being 'small' and were managed by their "creator" step-by-step through the process, plus the fact they were mostly adventurous and usually maverick-types. They made certain their guidelines were followed. The results were TOTAL FULL-CYCLE MANAGEMENT in it purest form.

The Industrial Age can be tracked as a growth phenomenon that encompassed the nation and the world. Twenty years into this new age of growth, 'all' were beginning to experience difficulty in efficiency and product quality. Failure to meet standards in existing and new products without production flaws and also timing failures prevailed.

In an effort to alleviate these problems, many systems where devised. I remember one of the most mistrusted during my early years in business was "Efficiency Experts" and often wondered if there were many recorded advantages during this period. Although, it did appear that something was at least being attempted by management to eradicate the problems.

Depending on the area of your expertise, I am convinced that you can name many programs that were devised to address this now growing and explosive problem. It seems that no business is completely void in production or completion problems. These problems often result in poor product quality and cost overruns.

There is presently a program called "Total Quality Management" that is being taught in some areas of industry, military installations, and private corporations in an attempt to eradicate the existing problems in project/production areas. This attempt to work together as a team has had its merits, but it is evident that there is still something missing.

The complexity of simplicity might explain why it took such a long time to assemble and process the problem to a conclusion. I am certain that many managers would get pieces of the puzzle, but could never fully comprehend what could solve this mystery to the satisfaction of every need within any management situation.

After much deliberation for a title for this manual, the fact that the conclusion of this phenomenon had eluded me for over twenty years was enough to call it "The Phantom in Management."

Section 4.

IDENTIFYING THE PHANTOM...................................

Notes:

IDENTIFYING THE PHANTOM

Planning and scheduling has always been the backbone of every business as well as in our personal lives. We must have adequate planning and scheduling to accomplish the goals set before us. What we need to have encompassed in our understanding . . . is that as we grow and especially <u>WHEN</u> we multiply into a composite of departments, we must have a mechanism to monitor ALL progress and especially ALL deviations from the original plan. More importantly, this knowledge must be reported systematically to ALL involved. If not, we can trace the breakdown of communications to each of those deviations.

Throughout our nation and the world there are numerous businesses. Thus, my dilemma is . . . HOW to write a scenario that would fit each type or occasion for the reader to grasp the connection to THEIR individual needs. It seemed only logical that I give the "phantom" a name that could fit any situation, explain the duties, and give an example of a Job Description.

To give the "phantom" a name would seem like a very simple task. Actually, I spent many months pondering over the perfect name. It is important for you to understand that the name or title must reflect no power over anyone. Yet, this person has great value to everyone.

This person must have particular attributes . . . dependable, responsible, has an understanding of scheduling and knowledgeable in full-cycle management techniques. Without these attributes, it would be difficult for the "phantom" to carry out the role as coordinator of progress and deviations from the manager's schedule. This person must have the ability to communicate to the proper person(s) or department(s)…(1) what is due (according to the information that was originally given), (2) when it is due, (3) when it is late, changed, or completed, and (4) compiles all records of reports given to them. This person must keep all records that are received that would explain each deviation as well as restart the scheduling process.

During this search, it occurred to me that the name 'watchdog' would leave no doubt of the person's responsibility, but that seemed degrading and would to any professional. I finally decided that most would agree that we can live with the name "COMPREHENSIVE COORDINATOR." But, ONLY if we are careful to explain the meaning as it adequately defines our use of this title. In the choice of 'COMPREHENSIVE,' the meaning I locked onto was INCLUSIVE…taking everything into account. In the choice of 'COORDINATOR,' it was to bring into proper order or relation, to adjust (by notifying and making adjustments as instructed).

The Comprehensive Coordinator is only in charge or responsible for communications as they track the schedule that has been presented. They report any changes and keep the schedule updated and current at all times. This person must be the historian of all reports that have justified the project, the deviations, as well as completion records. This centralizes all project schedules and final results.

When management chooses to give portions of the project schedule to more than one person, you NO LONGER have a 'Comprehensive Coordinator,' but individual coordinators. Only when the person is given control over ALL aspects of the project scheduling to MONITOR, do they become your 'Comprehensive Coordinator.' The individual coordinators on projects are only over specific areas and report all transactions to the Comprehensive Coordinator.

Section 5.

SELECTING YOUR COORDINATOR..........................

Notes:

SELECTING YOUR COORDINATOR

In the section named "Identifying the Phantom," we touched on the duties of the Comprehensive Coordinator. In selecting your Comprehensive Coordinator, it should be noted that there are employees who are considered 'naturals.'

ATTRIBUTES OF A 'NATURAL'

They communicate ideas to help the department run more smoothly and are ready to try different approaches to accomplish this goal. It is a natural impulse for them to push ahead and expand their job duties by incorporating steps to alleviate problems. They are usually personable and complete their duties wide-open (100%+).

Most likely will discover unique ways to better communicate with others in the department, even willing to assist them in reorganizing. Their ability to focus on full-cycle management is their great 'natural gift,' in addition to the personality and expertise to carry the coordination of the activities to completion.

Their enthusiasm proceeds their actions - thus, they are usually well known and respected (by other employees and other departments). This 'natural' phenomenon is usually taken for granted when there is such an employee in the department. When this person moves on or resigns, problems will eventually spring up. Most of the time, management never links those problems to the absence of this valuable employee.

When hiring a new employee for this position, you obviously do not have an opportunity to observe their work habits. The clues will be present as you review their resume'. How did the applicant describe the duties of their last position? When clues flash out, keep a record to be used when you interview.

During the interview, set up scenarios in which the applicant would be able to describe how they would handle such a specific situation and why. From these descriptions, you should see reflections of their work history. That will help you decide if the applicant is a 'natural' or if they could be trained to understand the duties of a COMPREHENSIVE COORDINATOR. The following suggestions for your job description will be broad and you will, I am convinced, be able to expand these scenarios into your individual needs and terminology.

- The goal of the Comprehensive Coordinator is to follow scheduled duties to completion. This would be accomplished by verifying, documenting, reminding and reporting each scheduled date as it has been revised or completed. Reports any deviation(s) to the proper person(s) or department(s), places the project schedule 'on hold' awaiting a new or updated schedule. The Comprehensive

Coordinator keeps check on the progress at assigned intervals until the revised scheduled dates have been re-established.

- Must have the ability to follow oral and written directions, as well as understand how to formulate a follow-up system.

- Communication skills must include writing with the ability to adequately describe or inform persons or departments of due date deviations. Must be thorough as well as competent in the area of following a project to each scheduled completion date.

- The Comprehensive Coordinator should function according to your specific needs and could be involved in the daily operations of your business or be solely a person who follows the written word to the letter and reports to only those you specify. There is no wrong way to incorporate the Comprehensive Coordinator as long as they are aware of ALL transactions.

- The Comprehensive Coordinator must be able to keep adequate files of all reports to completion of the project. This is necessary for management to maintain a complete and comprehensive record of all actions on the project. You must have predetermined if you need the Comprehensive Coordinator to fulfill this historian-type function. The historian role would probably be needed in a research or multi-department organization.

- One great tool to assure the Comprehensive Coordinator does not have a power struggle within the department(s) or organization is to FULLY explain their SPECIFIC duties in the beginning. These duties should be emphasized as the ONLY area for which they will be responsible. Explaining that they will be evaluated strictly on those specific duties and how precisely they are carried out to the completion of the project. Any lag in communication on their part will most definitely affect their evaluations and salary increases.

Section 6.

PRACTICE SCENARIO.......................................

Notes:

PRACTICE SCENARIO

The "Practice Scenario" is going to be fictitious, but actually similar to situations which I have encounter throughout my private life and career.

As essential as the element of communication is for all facets of our life, very few of us will take the time to fully analyze our problems to incorporate a solution. Problem solving in today's society has become a lost art. I have briefly covered scenarios in Research, Local Government, and Human Services. This segment is going to cover a "Practice Scenario" using the FAMILY as an example.

Even though our culture can be described as the most technological in history, we have lost our ability to even monitor the basics – our own families. Think about it . . . we can explore the Internet and virtually become educated in most any area of interest, but many don't have a clue about how to solve the problems within the most important area of our lives (our families).

Our society has a crisis in the area of communications which can be addressed by areas or departments and bring about vast improvements, but the crisis cannot be addressed piece-meal or from the top down for a NATIONAL REVOLUTION in full-cycle management. To accomplish this awesome feat, it most begin at the root of our society (the family) and expand to the top.

Those who study HISTORY will be able to verify that as 'Nations' grow into a multi-layered entity – so does communication problems and confusion.

If we can begin to visualize what the missing link encompasses in its simplest format (the family), then you will develop a specific mind set and have the ability to recognize the missing link in all other areas of your life.

It is apparent that we have neglected to train in this mind set. My goal is to accomplish this – although, we can't wait for the next generation for trained personnel. Perhaps, this manual is the beginning – one reader at a time. The change in mind set (understanding the missing link in management), coupled with perseverance and dedication could bring about a drastic improvement within a reasonable time frame.

The instructions are very simple and easy to follow. This scenario is going to be divided into three parts.

- The first part will tell the scenario detailing many communication problems. Each problem area will be addressed in part two.

- The second part will have questions which I will answer for you. Also, this part will encompass the planning stage showing strategies to increase communications. The ultimate solution will be using a Comprehensive Coordinator to bring about internal and external communications. Each of the corrected areas will then be incorporated into the scenario found in part three.

- While reviewing part three, you will notice an asterisk (*) before each area that has been affected by the correction. You will begin assimilating the needed changes and even anticipating the missing link as you read this scenario.

THE FAMILY SCENARIO

Part One:

We begin this scenario on Friday morning with the Jackson family of five. Shirley and Frank Jackson are the proud parents of Jeff (15), Chad (10), and Julie (4). This Friday began like every other Friday morning – a complete state of confusion.

Shirley was the Administrative Assistant to the Principal at Clover Middle School and pressure was mounting for the school to meet the SOL minimum level by next month. Shirley had reminded everyone involved of the State Examiners visit. However, she had not recorded the date on her home calendar and . . . there was no one to watch Julie after 3:00. She asked Frank to call his sister and his immediate reply was, "Shirley, you're going to make me late for the train." She yelled, "Chad, please call Aunt Carol and ask her to pick up Julie after school and take her to Day Care." I forgot to pick up my suit from the cleaners yesterday, so I have to pull something together quickly. OK, Chad replied – Aunt Carol was excited at the thought of visiting with her niece and happily agreed.

Chad was the most dependable of the three children, but he was in the middle of the 'literal' stage. If you tell him anything or pass on facts – you must make sure your 't's are crossed and you 'i's dotted. It's the only language this age group understands. Frank, a promising young lawyer in the City, was moving along very well this morning and already had finished his first cup of coffee – he was sure everything would be better from here on out. Frank asked Chad to bring him the folder off the desk. Chad walked back into the room with "a" folder and Frank said, "Just put it in my briefcase." Thanks!

Frank yelled from the downstairs bathroom – "Jeff, you had better be up!" Jeff, recognized this as the 'last-straw-call' and jumped up and into his yesterday jeans (but did take time for a clean shirt). As usual, Jeff's books were scattered upstairs and down which took a few minutes to retrieve. Mom, Jeff called "I need $15.00 for my soccer picture." Shirley went spastic – "Jeff, why are you telling me this now?" I'll have to write you a check – will they take it? Hurry, bring me the checkbook out of my briefcase.

Julie was her usual cheerful four-year-old self and decided to be a big girl and dress all-by-herself. Some of her clothes were still downstairs, so she wore what she could find in her dresser. Then she remembered that she had placed her tooth under her pillow last night and ran to see how much money the tooth fairy had given her. Julie let out a scream that brought everyone into her bedroom . . . they were certain she had been terribly injured. "What's wrong?" everyone said at once. "The tooth fairy took my tooth and didn't give me any money," she said. Shirley looked at Frank with eyes of stone – they both knew what happened…Shirley asked Frank to put a dollar under Julie's pillow last night while she had taken Julie out for her dance lessons (since they were a little late – she had forgotten the date change). At four years old, you can do a 'slight of hand' – Frank said, "Look it fell out on the floor." Little Julie squealed with joy. Once again, everyone started their harried attempt to get out of the house.

Shirley reminded everyone that they had fifteen minutes before it would be time to leave. At this point, Shirley had to completely redress Julie – which was a chore in itself. Shirley asked Chad to find Julie's book bag, then she gathered her briefcase, Julie, and yelled back at Frank to feed the dog. Oh, don't forget to pick up Jeff after practice – I will be in a meeting at school. "Come on Chad, we are going to be late."

Frank, mumbling under his breath, snatched a can of dog food down from the cabinet. Finally, He and Jeff scampered out the door. There is another "catch" – Frank didn't hear Shirley's comment about picking up Jeff after soccer.

As he began to calm down, he remembered that he didn't check to see if Chad had put everything in the briefcase. He said, "Jeff, open my briefcase and show me what Chad put in there." I only see an empty file folder. What . . . and he quickly turned the car around to go retrieve his "briefing" for his morning court case. After dropping Jeff off at school, Frank just barely had time to park the car and race to the train.

Well, the balance of the day went without a hitch for everyone until it was time to return home. Frank still had one more episode which had been left over from his morning fiasco – picking up Jeff from the soccer game on the way home from work.

Frank made his way off the train – looking at his watch, he realized that he would be the first to arrive at home today. I could handle a nap before the troops arrive.

After speaking to several of his neighbors, he threw his coat on a chair and took the paper and a drink out to the pool for little R and R. He didn't have his cell phone with him and couldn't hear the phone from the patio – Jeff had tried several times to reach him. Jeff then called his mother (she was still in her meeting) and said the coach needed to leave and Dad hadn't arrived to pick him up. Shirley said, "Jeff, ask the coach if he would have time to drop you off here at the school." Luckily, he could. Needless to say, Shirley's meeting was downhill after that phone call. She didn't know whether to be worried or angry!

They all arrived safely from school, but were anxious to check on Frank. When he learned of the mixup, he just shook his head.

You know, I have had about all I can stand of these disastrous mornings and communication problems. Every other day, we seem to be leaving someone. This is not safe! And, everybody is stressed through the roof. There are going to be extreme changes at our house, I promise you this! We will talk about this problem tomorrow morning. I want everyone present for a "family meeting" after breakfast. Don't make any plans!

Part Two:

A. RECOGNIZING THE FAMILY CRISIS

Frank called Jack, one of his closes friends, and they talked for a very long time. He explained the problems he and Shirley were experiencing with their family. Jack, he said, "with this much stress on any given day, I really don't know if our children or our marriage will survive; we have to make drastic changes soon." He then preceded to relate much of the "Friday morning fiasco" to Jack.

Jack listened patiently, then tried to interject a little humor into the conversation and laughingly said. "Who do you think is dropping the ball?" After a few thoughtful minutes, Frank replied – "all of us at one time or another." They both gave a little laugh – Frank said, "If I wasn't so upset and stressed, I could probably see where our life would make a great sitcom." Although, while you're living it, it's not funny!

Jack gave a heavy sigh, then proceeded to instruct Frank to buy a Calendar and get everybody's schedules listed by day. Frank – a little impatiently – blurred out, "Jack, do you really think writing everyone's schedule down on a calendar is going to solve my problem?" Just as impatiently, Jack said, "absolutely not!"

Frank, I have five directives for you and Shirley to complete by Sunday afternoon. I'll be by the house in just a few minutes to bring you and Shirley a manual to read tonight – don't grown so . . . it's actually a good hour's reading. I'll be over on Sunday, will three o'clock be a good time for you? Frank said, "as busy as you are, if you can fit us into your schedule, you better believe its great for us." Jack replied, "Trust me, things are going to get better." Frank, get Shirley on the line and I'll give her the directives at the same time.

❑ First Directive – Read the manual "The Phantom in Management" (both of you read this manual).

❑ Second Directive – Purchase a Calendar with large daily blocks. Take all of the family's schedules and fill in each day by TIME (completing their daily, weekly, and monthly schedules). Leave enough space for additional scheduled appointments. (This is assuming you already have a Budget Calendar – if not, purchase 2 Calendars and we will discuss this when I arrive on Sunday.)

❑ Third Directive – I am assuming also that you already have a BUDGET and are operating within the limits of your budget. Only if all aspects of your time and finances are correctly planned can you hope to bring about control of your family. If you don't, at least pull together a Budget Calendar by Sunday.

❑ Fourth Directive – Purchase a small kitchen-size blackboard or an ink board (erasable) that also has a cork board. This will be your DAILY DUTIES and NOTES TO THE FAMILY roster. Each member will review this daily – retrieving their messages and checking off their duties as they have been completed.

❑ Fifth Directive – Shirley will need to write a synopsis of your "terrible Friday." The two of you try to remember the order of every incident as it occurred. You might want to include "what you were thinking" at the time.

B. COMPLETING THE ASSIGNMENT

FIRST DIRECTIVE

Shirley and Frank completed "The Phantom in Management" by 10:30 Saturday night. They were amazed at their new insight into many of their problems, not only their family's crisis, but discussed areas in Shirley's and Frank's offices which needed the 1, 2, 3, & 4-step concept incorporated into the daily routines.

Shirley said, "Actually, it's frightening how disconnected we are as a family." We are so fortunate that nothing tragic has occurred because of our communication problems. Also, these problems most likely can explain many of the children's problems at school. There have probably been many positive opportunities missed.

To complete this first directive, we need to apply the 1, 2, 3, & 4-step concept.

STEP 1.

Shirley and Frank realized their family was disconnected and the missing link was SOMEONE to follow all of the schedules of each member of the family. They needed to incorporate a "Comprehensive Coordinator." The Calendar showing time and dates would not alleviate the problems – there must be PERSON to follow schedule.

STEP 2.

When we became a two-paycheck family, no one stepped in to assume the scheduling and coordinating of the family. This was previously performed by the Shirley. Mostly, it was left up to each individual to make everyone aware of their schedules and any deviations. No one was assigned to coordinate 'all' schedules into a composite. This left the family disconnected.

STEP 3.

After much deliberation, it was decided that they would make up a Calendar of weekly schedules of appointments and formulate a DAILY DUTIES SCHEDULE which will be posted on a ROSTER for each to follow. Then they would appoint someone as the family "Comprehensive Coordinator."

STEP 4.

Once we have established a "Comprehensive Coordinator" for the family, our schedules will be monitored completely by this person. Others may have specific duties, but this PERSON must be aware of all schedules, changes, or deviations – and keep all of the family updated on each.

During the late night review of their family's crisis, they followed the manual's instructions and began a process that would help them decide who would be best qualified to fulfill this important role.

They followed the "Job Description" suggestions in the manual to discover the most appropriate person to assume the duties of the Comprehensive Coordinator for the family.

They listed the names in the family across a page and then proceeded to mark off their abilities using an "X" where it was appropriate.

Frank	Shirley	Jeff	Chad	Julie
	X			
X	X			
X	X			
X	X			
	X			
X	X			

It is apparent that Shirley is the closest to a 'Natural' and would be the obvious choice to be the Comprehensive Coordinator. Frank could perform the duties, but since he has had an assistant to complete the follow-up on all his schedules, it would be more difficult for him to adjust. The children were considered on each issue, but haven't the experience to carry out the paperwork, scheduling, or have the ability to stay focused on the objective. Although, being involved with the steps of the process will give them a chance to observe how this type of full-cycle management works. This will formulate a full-cycle management lifestyle – a valuable education in itself!

SECOND DIRECTIVE

Frank and Shirley stopped on the way home from church to make the necessary purchases to be ready when Jack arrived this afternoon. They needed two (2) Calendars (one for Family and one for Budget), and a looseleaf notebook for the Comprehensive Coordinator to compile all her information.

THIRD DIRECTIVE

Since Shirley had been chosen as the family's Comprehensive Coordinator, she went to her office and using the children's schedules, Frank's and her work schedules and the Budget…she completed the Family's Calendar and the Budget Calendar for the MONTH. On the Budget Calendar, she went through the entire year to record quarterly, 6 months, and yearly due dates for Car Insurance, Taxes, Personal Property, Licenses and Mortgage Insurance.

FOURTH DIRECTIVE

Shirley went to retrieve her notes from the telephone conversation with Jack, and checked to see what else they needed to complete before 3:00. There it was – need an ink erasable board with one side cork to be used as a DAILY DUTIES AND NOTES Roster. Also, that she should make a list of specific duties for everyone for each day (for one week). She quickly typed out a list and then left in a rush to pick up the erasable board before Jack arrived.

FIFTH DIRECTIVE

Frank began typing a rough draft of the "terrible Friday" while Shirley went to the store. When Shirley returned, she reviewed his draft and added a few comments and had it ready when Jack arrived.

C. PLANNING SESSION

Jack arrived promptly at 3:00 o'clock and immediately began to review the Directives with Shirley and Frank. I am very pleased! It is evident that you now have a handle on your problems. Also, I feel confident that you have grasped the concept of the missing link in management.

Jack said, "Are there any questions about the Directives?" Frank said, "Shirley is going to be our Family Comprehensive Coordinator. After reviewing our Budget, we both felt that we can afford a housekeeper once a week. This would give Shirley the additional time she needs to fulfill this responsibility. What is your 'take' on this idea?" Jack agreed that this would be a very positive move.

Jack said, "I really don't have too much to add." You have accomplished a great deal this week end. I would suggest the following:

- Work up a Job Description for Shirley. It's important that every aspect of her duties is written down – then she will have a guide to insure that she doesn't drop the ball on any of the families schedules. (See attached Job Description.)
- Also, I would suggest you erase the DETAILED information on your FAMILY CALENDAR about your work schedules and Bills due. (You have this information detailed on your BUDGET CALENDAR and on your WORK SCHEDULES.) Use asterisks beside your due date for Bills (**). This clears up your "Family Calendar" for your daily schedules and appointments. (See attached Family Calendar.)

- We need to review your synopsis of the "terrible Friday" and number each incident. Then we will use your 'new system' and include the Comprehensive Coordinator's duties to rewrite this scenario. (See attached "terrible Friday" worksheet synopsis.)

- After completion of these suggestions, you will be ready to hold your FAMILY PLANNING SESSION. Explain what you think needs to be done and how you have organized each step – then ask for their input and questions. If they have legitimate suggestions, incorporate them. Make sure they understand your commitment to this change and that they will be expected to fulfill their commitments also. (See attached "Family Planning Session" synopsis.)

Jack said, "If you don't need me to complete these suggestions, I really need to get home – we have visitors arriving at 6:00 o'clock." Frank said, "Thank you so much for your help and I'll get in touch with you at some point next week to let you know how we are doing."

JOB DESCRIPTION

The Comprehensive Coordinator (Shirley) will organize a MONTHLY CALENDAR for the family – showing dates and appointments. Also, she will monitor the Work Schedule Calendar and the Budget Calendar daily for any changes or appointments and note with asterisks any due dates and appointments on the FAMILY CALENDAR as a reminder to check these Calendars for particulars. The Family Calendar will be formulated at the beginning of each month. The Calendar will be reviewed on a daily basis. She will make changes or cancellations as needed – informing each member of the family about these changes. She will place a note explaining the change under the person's name on the NOTE Board.

Each member must inform the C.C. as soon as they have a change in schedule or a new activity for inclusion on the CALENDAR. Anyone at anytime can check the Calendar (for their own schedule or to find anyone in the family), but must not make ANY corrections or additions – ONLY Shirley can write anything – or change anything on the CALENDAR! They may write her a note and place it under her name on the NOTES Board.

When the C.C. makes any additions or changes – each person in the family must be notified as soon as possible. Notes can be placed under their names on the NOTES board or hand delivered – but must be documented.

The C.C. must formulate a DAILY DUTIES ROSTER each Saturday. The duties will be posted on the Ink Board under DAILY DUTIES each day. These are specific duties each will perform throughout the week. Each duty needs to be checked off as it is completed – Shirley will be monitoring these daily. And if someone hasn't completed their duties, she must remind them. There will be consequences if this happens too often without good reason.

May 2004

* Work related
** Budget related (Bills Due)-Check Budget Calendar

Sun	Mon	Tue	Wed	Thu	Fri	Sat
						1 C.C./Cal.&Daily Duties 9:30 Chad/Soccer
2 (Everybody) 9:00 S.S./church 12:00 Lunch/ Grandma's	3 7:30 Exit (all) * 8:00 Dad/Mtg **	4 7:30 Exit (all) * 11:00 Mom/Mtg 6:00 Chad/Gm	5 7:30 Exit (all) 10:00 Julie/ Dentist-Mom takes 6:30 Jeff/Gm	6 7:30 Exit (all) * 9:00 Dad/Crt Jeff $15/Mom/p.u.suit 6:30 Julie/Dance	7 7:30 Exit (all) * 11:00 Dad/Brf * 10:00 Mom/Mtg 4:30 Dad/p.u.Jeff	8 9:30 Chad/Soccer 2:00 Julie/Party C.C./Daily Duties 8:00 Visitors
9 (Everybody) 9:00 S.S./Church 12:30 Luncheon/ for Grandpa	10 7:30 Exit (all) * 9:00 Dad/Crt * 11:00 Mom/Mtg 7:30 CHAD/PTO	11 7:30 Exit (all) 11:30 Chad/ Dentist/Dad 6:00 Chad/Gm	12 7:30 Exit (all) * 11:00 Dad/Client 6:30 Jeff/Gm	13 7:30 Exit (all) 9:00 Dad/Crt 6:30 Julie/Dance	14 7:30 Exit (all) * 11:30 Mom/Mtg 3:00 Jeff/Game	15 9:30 Chad/Soccer C.C./Daily Duties
16 (Everybody) 9:00 S.S./Church 3:00 Jack/Mtg	17 7:30 Exit (all) **	18 7:30 Exit (all) 6:00 Chad/Gm	19 7:30 Exit (all) 6:30 Jeff/Gm	20 7:30 Exit (all) * 9:00 Dad/Crt 6:30 Julie/Dance	21 7:30 Exit (all) 3:00 Jeff/Game **	22 C.C./Daily Duties 2:00 Wedding
23 (Everybody) 9:00 S.S./Church 12:30 Guests for lunch	24 7:30 Exit (all) * Dad/Mtg.	25 7:30 Exit (all 6:00 Chad/Gm	26 7:30 (all) ** 6:30 Jeff/Gm	27 7:30 Exit (all)	28 7:30 Exit (all)	29 9:30 Chad/Soccer C.C./Daily Duties
30 (Everybody) 9:00 S.S./Church	31 7:30 Exit (all)					

DAILY DUTIES ROSTER

	Monday	Tuesday	Wednesday	Thursday	Friday	Saturday	Sunday
SHIRLEY	Ck/Duties & Calendar	Same	Same	Same	Same	Same	Same
	Breakfast	Dinner	Breakfast	Dinner	Breakfast	Dinner	Breakfast
FRANK	Dresses/ Julie	Same	Same	Same	Same	Same	Same
	Dinner	Breakfast	Dinner	Breakfast	Dinner	Breakfast	Dinner
JEFF	Unloads Dishwasher	Same	Same	Same	Same	Same	Same
	Feeds dog – Morning Evening	"	"	"	"	"	"
CHAD	Clears table - Morning/ Evening	Same	Same	Same	Same	Same	Same
	Takes out the Trash	"	"	"	"	"	"
	Check/on books, etc., for morning	"	"	"	"	"	"

55

JULIE	Gets her	Same	Same	Same	Same	Same	Same
	Book bag						
	Sets table -	"	"	"	"	"	"
	Morning/						
	Evening						

SHIRLEY – Daily Duties Roster Rotates Weekly (Begins new Roster on Monday).

"Terrible Friday" Synopsis

We begin this scenario on Friday morning with the Jackson family of five. Shirley and Frank Jackson are the proud parents of Jeff (15), Chad (10), and Julie (4). This Friday began like every other Friday morning – a complete state-of-confusion.

Shirley was the Administrative Assistant to the Principal at Clover Middle School and pressure was mounting for the school to meet the SAT minimum level by next month. Shirley had reminded everyone involved of the State Examiners visit, but had not recorded the date on her Family Calendar. (1)

(The C.C. would have checked this off her WORK CALENDAR and it would have been on the FAMILY CALENDAR.) and . . . there was no one to watch Julie after 3:00 o'clock, (2)

(This would have already been scheduled by the C.C. when the Calendar was updated.)

she asked Frank to call his sister and his immediate reply was, "Shirley, you're going to make me late for the train." She yelled, Chad, please call Aunt Carol and ask her to pick up Julie after school and take her to Day Care." I have to find something to wear because I forgot to pick up my suit from the cleaners yesterday, (3)

(The C.C. would have this noted on her Family Calendar from her Work Calendar and this would not have been forgotten.)

I will have to pull something together quickly. OK, Chad replied – Aunt Carol was excited at the thought of visiting with her niece and happily agreed.

Chad was the most dependable of the three children, but he was in the middle of the 'literal' stage. If you tell him anything or pass on facts – you must make sure your 't's are crossed and your 'i's dotted. It's the only language they understand. Frank, who was a promising young lawyer, was moving along very well this morning and already had finished his first cup of coffee – he was sure everything would be better from here on out. He called out to Chad – bring me the folder off my desk. (4)

(The C.C. would have made sure everyone had their materials downstairs and ready to go last night.)

Chad walked back into the room with "a" folder and Frank said, "Just put it in my briefcase. Thanks!"

Frank yelled from the downstairs bathroom – "Jeff, you had better be up!" Jeff, recognized this as the 'last-straw-call' and jumped up and into his yesterday jeans (but did take time for a clean shirt). As usual, Jeff's books were scattered upstairs and down which took a few minutes to retrieve. (5)

(This also would have been handled the night before by the C.C.)

Mom, Jeff called, "I need $15.00 for my soccer picture." Shirley went spastic – "Jeff, why are you telling me this now?" (6)

(The C.C. would have recorded this on the Calendar and had the check (or cash) ready for Jeff.)

I'll have to write you a check – I surely hope they will accept it. Hurry, bring me the checkbook out of my briefcase.

Julie was her usual cheerful four-year old self and decided to be a big girl and dress all-by-herself. Some of her clothes were still downstairs, so she wore what she could find in her dresser. (7)

(The C.C. would have everyone's clothes ready – this is going to be a family project on Saturday.)

Then she remembered that she had placed her tooth under her pillow last night and ran so see how much money the tooth fairy had given her. Julie let out a scream that brought everyone into her bedroom . . . they were certain she had been terribly injured. "What's wrong?" everyone said at once. "The tooth fairy took my tooth and didn't give me any money," she said. Shirley looked at Frank with eyes of stone – they both knew what happened…Shirley asked Frank to put a dollar under

Julie's pillow last night while she took Julie to her dance lessons. At four years old, you can do a 'slight-of-hand' – Frank said, "Look it fell on the floor." Little Julie squealed with joy! Once again, everyone started their harried attempt to get out of the house. (8)

(The C.C. would have taken care of this ahead of time – or assigned the job to someone else and then checked to make sure it had been done.)

Frank said, "This wouldn't have happened . . . but you are always late for everything." (9)

(They were late for the lesson because Shirley didn't make a note of the change of date.)

Shirley reminded everyone that they had fifteen minutes before it would be time to leave. At this point, Shirley had to completely re-dress Julie – which was a chore in itself. Shirley asked Chad to find Julie's book bag, then she gathered her briefcase, Julie, and yelled back at Frank to feed the dog. (10)

(The C.C. would have someone assigned a "Daily Duty" to feed the dog.)

Oh, don't forget to pick up Jeff after practice – I will be in a meeting at school. Shirley said, "Come on Chad, we are going to be late."

Frank, mumbled under his breath and snatched a can of dog food down from the cabinet. Finally, Frank and Jeff scampered out the door. There is another "catch" – Frank didn't hear Shirley's comment about picking up Jeff after soccer. (11)

(The C.C. would have this change on the Calendar and someone assigned to pick him up.)

As Frank began to calm down, he remembered that he didn't check to see if Chad had put everything in the briefcase. He said, "Jeff, open my briefcase and show me what Chad put in there." Jeff said, "I only see an empty file folder." What . . . and Frank quickly turned the car around to go retrieve his "briefing" for his morning court case. After dropping Jeff off at school, Frank just barely had time to park the car and race to the train.

Well, the balance of the day went without a hitch, but Frank had one more episode which had been left over from this morning's fiasco. Frank didn't know he was suppose to pick up Jeff from the soccer game on the way home from work.

After speaking to several of his neighbors, he threw his coat on a chair and took the paper and a drink out to the patio for a little R and R. He didn't have his cell phone with him and couldn't hear the phone from the patio – Jeff had tried several times to reach him. Jeff then called his mother (she was still in her meeting) and told her that the coach needed to leave and Dad hadn't arrived. Shirley told Jeff to ask the Coach if he would have time to drop him off here at the school. The Coach agreed. Needless to say, Shirley's meeting went downhill after that phone call. She didn't know whether to be worried or angry. They all arrived safely from school, but were anxious to check on Frank.

(All of the above scenario would never had occurred!)

You know, I have had about all I can stand of these disastrous mornings and communication problems. Every other day, we seem to be leaving someone. This is not safe! Also, everybody is stressed through the roof. There are going to be extreme changes at our house, I promise you this! We are going talk about this problem tomorrow morning. I want everyone present for "a family meeting" after breakfast. Don't make any plans!

D. FAMILY PLANNING SESSION

Frank decided to represent the "moderator" for this Planning Session. Shirley decided to take notes – thought it might be an instrument to assist her in the days ahead.

They began the meeting by reiterating their terrible Friday morning. It was still very vivid in everyone's mind. After reading the first synopsis, Frank started to explain what they had been planned, so far.

Shirley handed everyone an "outline" to follow the progression of the meeting. She made sure that they understood that their input was valuable. Also, gave them permission to speak openly (but calmly) about any aspect of the meeting.

EXPLAINING THE MISSING LINK IN MANAGEMENT

Shirley explained very briefly what had been missing in their FAMILY every since she had returned to work. She and Frank apologized to the children for making them feel that they were responsible for all the stress that occurred in their home. It's important for you to understand that we were disconnected and this brings about neglect and confusion (even in the most loving households).

Frank began the meeting by reiterating that they were a part of the PLANNING and EXECUTION of the "Family Goal." The Family Goal is to be CONNECTED in all areas of the family. Everyone will have to participate for this GOAL to be successful. I guess you know, this does NOT mean we will operate as a Democracy, I'm still 'DAD' and have the last word, but you may have a voice in the PLANNING. Also, you may ask questions about anything you do not understand.

Frank said, "After reading a management training manual 'The Phantom in Management,' our problems become clear." Lets follow the outline Mom just gave you.

OUTLINE

❑ The first order of business was to select someone to follow all of us in our schedules throughout the day.

❑ After answering a short questionnaire, it was apparent your Mom would be the family "Comprehensive Coordinator".

❑ We are going to call her "The C.C." as we explain the rest of the OUTLINE.

❑ The C.C. has completed a Family Calendar and included all of schedules under each day of the week. Shirley passed each one a copy to review. She will help us stay on track – HOWEVER, your part is to always keep her informed when you have a change in your schedules. This is extremely important and if you do not, the C.C. cannot keep all of us on track. You will be held to this responsibility.

❑ The C.C. also will give you duties on a weekly basis and Shirley passed out a copy of the weekly DAILY DUTIES ROSTER for their review. These duties will be posted on an INK BOARD each week beside your name. You will check off the duties as you have completed them. Make it a habit to check the BOARD often – 1) to remind you of your daily duties, 2) to check off duties completed, and 3) watch for any changes that the C.C. may have written. She will inform you of changes – but she needs your total concern and assistance – she has a tremendous task to help all of us to stay on schedule. The other side of the BOARD is for notes (telephone messages received, changes in appointments, reminders, and even a nice message of encouragement (sometimes).

❑ Points are calculated at the end of each week. You will receive a $25.00 allowance for you participation – but for every missed duty completion – or, neglect to inform the C.C. about your changed schedule, there will be a $5.00 penalty (unless it is beyond your control - the C.C. will make this determination.) The plus side – anyone who keeps the duties completed and all changes reported for the entire month will receive a $25.00 Bonus for their efforts.

❑ The C.C. will make all changes on the Roster – but you may remove your notes from the NOTES Board. These notes will appear under everyone's name as indicated – this includes Mom and Dad.

❑ We are going to have a FAMILY NIGHT each week – most of the time it will be Friday – but this is subject to change (we have to consider everyone's schedules). There will be special food and fun or maybe even a trip out together. Everyone gets to plan a night…food and special events.

❑ Also, on Saturday there will be at least a two-hour family work session – mostly for helping with the laundry (folding and putting away clothes). Except for keeping things put away, most of the cleaning will be done by our housekeeper – we have decided that MOM needs more help than the family can give. Since we want a less stressful life – all areas of our life must be planned.

❑ Frank will continue to pay bills and keep the Budget on track – the C.C. will help by monitoring due dates and reminders on the weekly FAMILY CALENDAR (and NOTES when appropriate).

❑ Just for an eye-opener, we rewrote our "terrible Friday" – this will help you understand how we have eliminated most of our confusion by planning and incorporation a C.C. for our family.

❑ The family has the same schedule and duties, but we are now connected and support each other for a more stress free and organized/contented life style. Now we can see if anyone drops the ball – and fix it before the entire family has to suffer.

❑ This system will begin on MONDAY – any more questions? Jeff said, "No, but I already feel a sense of relief and like you Dad, I was very frustrated with the stress here at home."

Part Three:

The following re-enactment of the family's "Terrible Friday" will include the corrective measure which the FAMILY has incorporated into their life style. The corrective measures are listed as follows:

• The missing link in the family was a COMPREHENSIVE COORDINATOR and Shirley was selected to fulfill this role. Also, decided to hire a Housekeeper to free more time for Shirley to complete her added duties.

• Planning – Frank and Shirley planned the FAMILY GOALS.

• Budget – Added a Budget Calendar to their Budget Process.

- Schedule – Completed a Family Calendar with everyone's schedule recorded. This is the simplest form of a follow-up system.

- Organized a DAILY DUTIES Roster and Notes Board.

- Organized a POINTS SYSTEM to encourage involvement and interest.

- Planned a FAMILY NIGHT each week – this is vital to family bonding and cooperation.

- RESULTS – The following re-enactment of last Friday morning will demonstrate the positive results of incorporating a Comprehensive Coordinator and Family Planning Goals.

TERRIFIC FRIDAY SYNOPSIS

We begin this scenario on Friday morning with the Jackson family of five. Shirley and Frank Jackson are the proud parents of Jeff (15), Chad (10), and Julie (4). This Friday began differently than any other Friday morning – smooth sailing!

Shirley was the Administrative Assistant to the Principal at Clover Middle School and pressure was mounting for the school to meet the SOL minimum level by next month. *Shirley had reminded everyone involved of the State Examiner's visit, included this date on the family Calendar, and had coordinated the family's involvement and covered all the bases. The feeling of being in control was indescribable – Shirley checked the Calendar, Daily Duties, and the NOTES board to make sure everyone had read them.

*Frank had called Aunt Carol – left a note to confirm this schedule for the C.C. (Carol would pick up Julie and take her to Day Care – the C.C. would need to pick her up after her scheduled meeting), *he had picked up Shirley's suit at the cleaners, and *confirmed that he would pick up Jeff after school. *Oh, I put a $1.00 under Julie's pillow for the Tooth Fairy, thanks for the note!

*Shirley had placed Jeff's $15.00 for his soccer pictures in an envelope and put it on the NOTES board for him to take to school today for his soccer picture. Jeff, Shirley said, "Bring me a receipt for the payment."

*Shirley called to the family that she had breakfast ready. *Chad made sure last night that everybody had "all" their books, book bags, and briefcases on the credenza (*with all necessary materials inside), and had taken out the trash. Jeff unloaded the dishwasher (*he got up early – trying to win the monthly $25.00 to go on a soccer tournament) and *had already fed the dog. *Frank had dressed Julie (since the clothes were in the dresser in groups by days – it went smoothly). *Julie was already downstairs and so happy to be setting the table and trying to decide what to buy with her $1.00 the tooth fairy had left under the pillow.

The C.C. reminded everyone to check their NOTES for the day and they "all" had to leave in fifteen minutes. Chad said, "I think everything is ready – except I still need to clear the table and put the dishes in the dishwasher."

Frank just stood at the door for a few minutes as everyone headed out to the car – what a terrific Friday, he thought. This is going to work!

That evening at their "family night" Frank and Shirley gave the entire family great marks on their morning efforts! It was Franks turn to fix dinner for their special night – it was Pizza. They all went out to pick up dinner and choose a movie.

Frank called Jack before the night was over and gave him a full report. Shirley and I owe you a great debt of thanks! Jack just remarked – that's what friends are all about! Frank said, "because you made time for us and showed us what was missing, we are now a functioning family." This has been a life changing experience for us all!

Section 7

CONCLUSION.......................................

Notes:

CONCLUSION

This very simplistic approach to "The Missing Link in Management" has been a journey into the past for me. Your understanding of this phenomenon will impact how you view full-cycle management in every facet of your life in the future.

As you realize now, most areas of business as well as our personal lives have a planned schedule, but most do not have a PERSON assigned to track and report each step or delay in the process. Your management genius, I am convinced, has spontaneously visualized how to customize this newly acquired knowledge to your specific missing link in management.

It would be interesting if I could be present and if I were, my question to you would be, "Could you now see the simplicity of the 1, 2, 3, and 4-step method outlined at the end of the INTRODUCTION?" For your quick access I will reiterate:

1. You will understand the simplicity of the missing link.
2. You will recognize your management area that is missing this facet.
3. You will formulate a plan to incorporate this link as soon as possible.

4. You will need to make the determination if you have a person on board or need to hire.

The discovery of "The Missing Link in Management" will be an insight into Quality Control and will automatically put you into an entirely different category of managers. The irony of this managerial style is that those around you will probably not have a clue to the reason for your success.

REFLECTIONS

While editing "The Phantom in Management," it occurred to me that over the last year there were vivid examples of many disastrous outcomes in our local, national, and international community which could possibly have been diverted had there been an active COMPREHENSIVE COORDINATOR position in each area and properly utilized. In the case of fraud, it is difficult to pull off scams when everyone is watching.

It appears that agencies, both local and federal are organizing committees to address the problems in communications (which must mean they suspect also that something is missing.) My thought was HOW do they plan to connect these individual agencies and if that is not in the scenario, I suspect "someone will drop the ball."

To those who have taken a few minutes of their day to share in my thoughts, I do honestly believe you were searching for an answer to "The Phantom in Management." It has been my intent to align your understanding with my own.

Only the giants in management who read this manual have the power to incorporate this missing link in management and bring about a much needed reform.

ABOUT THE AUTHOR

The author, Marjorie L. Ellis, has taken this opportunity to thank the many managers who contributed their genius and experience to training her in the "art" of management.

Her career began in retail even before she graduated. Long before her graduation day, her "natural" attributes were being recognized by teachers and won a full scholarship from Miller & Rhoads in retail as a buyer. Like many 'young' people - she decided marriage was more important and choose to marry a great guy, William H. Ellis, instead. They have two wonderful children (Bill and Tammy). She continued in her career before and after the children were born.

It is within her personality to be a "natural" Coordinator - this phenomenon is explained in 'The Phantom in Management.' She was given an awesome opportunity to excel in management by (what she considered to be) "intellectual" giants. Throughout her career, each manager afforded her the opportunity to be trained within the confines of their management expertise (Retail, Local and State Government, and Research). This included training courses in time management, writing, orientation in establishing goals, and various management training in Research and Local Government.

Her career escalated, resulting in speaking engagements, training opportunities, and ultimately to a business as a Consultant. The City offered her a contract to write the Policy and Procedure Manuals for Accounts Receivable, Accounts Payable, and the Refuse Department. This experience in the "interviewing process" led her career into another Consultant field.

This manual is a culmination of all her training and experience. She believes it to be an actual 25-year Pilot Program in various areas of Management. Specifically, the manual describes the missing link in management with a detailed step-by-step training program that could be grasped by most managers within an hour of reading.

www.ingramcontent.com/pod-product-compliance
Lightning Source LLC
Chambersburg PA
CBHW020341290526
45785CB00005B/2122